DEPOTS OF THE
UNDERGROUND RAILROAD

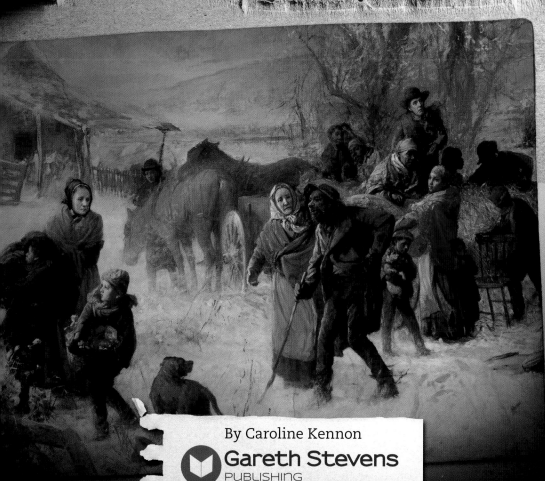

By Caroline Kennon

Gareth Stevens
PUBLISHING

Please visit our website, www.garethstevens.com. For a free color catalog of all our high-quality books, call toll free 1-800-542-2595 or fax 1-877-542-2596.

Library of Congress Cataloging-in-Publication Data

Names: Kennon, Caroline, author.
Title: Depots of the underground railroad / Caroline Kennon.
Description: New York : Gareth Stevens Publishing, 2017. | Series: Hidden history | Includes index.
Identifiers: LCCN 2016028254| ISBN 9781482457940 (pbk. book) | ISBN 9781482457957 (6 pack) | ISBN 9781482457964 (library bound book)
Subjects: LCSH: Underground Railroad–Juvenile literature. | Fugitive slaves–United States–History–19th century–Juvenile literature.
Classification: LCC E450 .K425 2017 | DDC 973.7/115–dc23
LC record available at https://lccn.loc.gov/2016028254

First Edition

Published in 2017 by
Gareth Stevens Publishing
111 East 14th Street, Suite 349
New York, NY 10003

Copyright © 2017 Gareth Stevens Publishing

Designer: Katelyn E. Reynolds
Editor: Therese Shea

Photo credits: Cover, p. 1 DcoetzeeBot/Wikipedia.org; cover, pp. 1–32 (tear element) Shahril KHMD/Shutterstock.com; cover, pp. 1–32 (background texture) cornflower/ Shutterstock.com; cover, pp. 1–32 (background colored texture) K.NarlochLiberra/ Shutterstock.com; cover, pp. 1–32 (photo texture) DarkBird/Shutterstock.com; cover, pp. 1–32 (notebook paper) Tolga TEZCAN/Shutterstock.com; p. 5 BrooklynMuseumBot/ Wikipedia.org; p. 7 (inset) Cliffswallow-vaulting/Wikipedia.org; pp. 7 (main), 11, 19, 21 Everett Historical/Shutterstock.com; p. 9 JA1BSR~commonswiki/Wikipedia.org; p. 10 Lotsofissues~commonswiki/Wikipedia.org; p. 13 Scewing/Wikipedia.org; p. 15 MGA73bot2/Wikipedia.org; p. 17 MPI/Getty Images; pp. 23, 25 courtesy of the Library of Congress; p. 27 (inset) Fastfission~commonswiki/Wikipedia.org; p. 27 (main) Daniel Case/Wikipedia.org; p. 29 WolfgangKaehler/LightRocket via Getty Images.

Printed in the United States of America

CPSIA compliance information: Batch #CW17GS: For further information contact Gareth Stevens, New York, New York at 1-800-542-2595.

CONTENTS

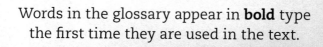

Words in the glossary appear in **bold** type
the first time they are used in the text.

ABOARD THE UNDERGROUND RAILROAD

In 1831, a Kentucky slave named Tice Davids swam across the Ohio River toward freedom. According to a story, Davids's owner watched as the slave disappeared at the edge of the river and said he must have "gone off on an underground railroad."

More than a decade later, newspapers in New York City and Boston, Massachusetts, used this term—the Underground Railroad—to describe how slaves had mysteriously escaped their owners. One report said that a slave "fell through into the under-ground railroad, and was carried along the subterranean [underground] passage on one of the steam cars." This wasn't the start of an actual railroad, but instead a massive effort by slaves and free people alike to secretly bring thousands of black slaves to freedom in the North.

REVEALED

The final destination for many slaves was Canada, which was often called the "Promised Land."

QUAKERS TO THE RESCUE

Some say that an organized system to help runaway slaves may have begun as early as the end of the 18th century. In 1786, George Washington complained that one of his runaway slaves was helped by a "society of Quakers, formed for such purposes." The Quakers were a religious group who were strongly and publicly against slavery. In the 1800s, the Quakers were a major force in running the Underground Railroad.

The Underground Railroad captured the imagination of artists, though they often drew upon real-life experiences.

NEXT STOP: FREEDOM

In America of the 18th and 19th centuries, ownership of slaves was common. Slaves were mostly descendants of Africans. After the American Revolution, northern states such as Pennsylvania and New York abolished slavery, but southern states such as Alabama and Mississippi retained it, largely because their economy depended on it. Wanting freedom, many enslaved people in the South attempted to escape north. They often required help getting there. This help took the shape of a hidden network of people and places leading to freedom.

As the term "Underground Railroad" became popular for the network, so did other terms relating to trains, such as "conductors," "passengers," and "depots." They were used to describe the individuals and locations in the Underground Railroad.

REVEALED

Secret codes were used by stationmasters, conductors, and everyone involved in helping slaves to freedom. Slaves themselves often used codes in song to communicate.

TRAIN TERMS

In the Underground Railroad, depots, or stations, were the homes and businesses where escaped slaves would stop to hide, sleep, and eat. Those who owned these locations and welcomed escaped slaves were called stationmasters. Individuals who contributed money or supplies to the network were called stockholders. The conductor was responsible for moving fugitive slaves from one station or depot to the next. Harriet Tubman was one of the most famous conductors.

Harriet Tubman

Cruelty towards slaves was common and often unpunished. Slave owners sometimes chained and whipped slaves.

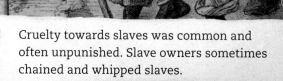

Many think both **abolitionists** and slave owners **exaggerated** the organization of the Underground Railroad to help their causes. In 1898, historian Wilbur H. Siebert published detailed maps of the supposed routes of the Underground Railroad. Despite this, historians now believe that it wasn't so neatly structured. Historian Eric Foner stated that the Underground Railroad was a "series of local networks . . . which together helped a substantial number of fugitives reach safety in the free states and Canada."

A majority of the individuals helping slaves to freedom were black, and most only knew of the local efforts to help slaves escape and not of the overall operation. The Underground Railroad succeeded because of the passion of these individual people at the local level, not necessarily because of a larger system of routes.

FREEDOM IS THE CURE FOR SLAVERY

In 1851, a doctor named Samuel Cartwright published his beliefs about a medical condition that he called "Drapetomania." It supposedly caused slaves to run away. The only "cures" were to either treat slaves kindly or whip them. Even though only a few thousand slaves escaped each year, these escapees—and those in the North who encouraged and aided the escapees—became a big concern for southern slave owners. They considered the slaves their stolen property.

REVEALED

While most Underground Railroad routes headed north, others led south to Mexico and the Caribbean.

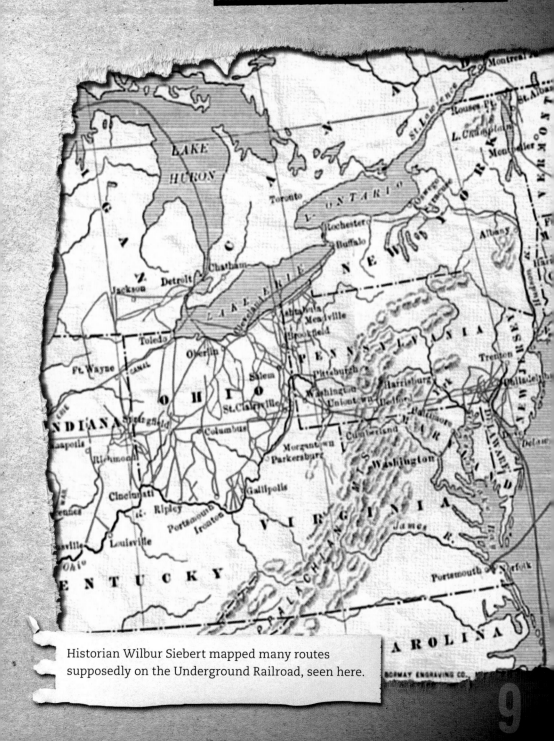

Historian Wilbur Siebert mapped many routes supposedly on the Underground Railroad, seen here.

TRANSFER AT THE NEXT DEPOT

Escaping to freedom wasn't easy. Slaves left their plantations in the middle of the night, sometimes led by a conductor who was pretending to be a slave, too. They often traveled 10 or 20 miles (16 or 32 km) until they reached a depot where they could rest safely. The fugitives then waited until the next stop could be notified and prepared for them. It was illegal for anyone to help these slaves in any way once they had escaped.

In 1850, the Fugitive Slave Act was passed. It required that all runaway slaves be returned to their masters. People who helped the slaves were supposed to be punished. The act also meant escaped slaves had to be hidden in free states, too.

CAUTION!!

COLORED PEOPLE

OF BOSTON, ONE & ALL,

You are hereby respectfully CAUTIONED and advised, to avoid conversing with the

Watchmen and Police Officers of Boston,

For since the recent ORDER OF THE MAYOR & ALDERMEN, they are empowered to act as

KIDNAPPERS

AND

Slave Catchers,

And they have already been actually employed in KIDNAPPING, CATCHING, AND KEEPING SLAVES. Therefore, if you value your LIBERTY, and the Welfare of the Fugitives among you, Shun them in every possible manner, as so many HOUNDS on the track of the most unfortunate of your race.

Keep a Sharp Look Out for KIDNAPPERS, and have TOP EYE open.

APRIL 24, 1851.

REVEALED

The Fugitive Slave Act was nicknamed the "Bloodhound Law." Sometimes dogs were used to track down slaves.

SLAVES IN DISGUISE

Sometimes runaway slaves had to use trains to travel longer distances or use boats to cross water. When slaves used these forms of transportation, they couldn't look like slaves or people would know they were fleeing slavery. Instead, they needed to look like free blacks, which meant wearing clothes that weren't worn or ragged. Both transportation and new clothing cost money. This money was often donated by generous individuals or raised by antislavery groups.

Slaves often had to escape from their owners in the dark and sometimes through rain and snow.

CONDUCTOR
TUBMAN

The Underground Railroad had many famous conductors and stationmasters. Probably the most well-known conductor was Harriet Tubman. She's said to have helped save over 300 slaves (though only 70 are known for sure). Tubman told Frederick Douglass, the escaped slave who became a famous abolitionist and writer, that she "never lost a single passenger" on her travels using the Underground Railroad.

Tubman was born a slave in Maryland in 1820 or 1821. In 1849, she became afraid that she would be sold, so she left her plantation on foot and walked to Pennsylvania. The next year, she went back to Maryland to get her sister and sister's children. On her third trip, she rescued her brother. Every time she got to safety, she felt the urge to return to save others.

REVEALED

Harriet Tubman was nicknamed "Moses," after the leader in the Bible who led his people out of slavery. Frederick Douglass said, "I know of no one who has willingly encountered more perils and hardships to serve our enslaved people."

HARRIET THE SPY

Harriet Tubman even worked as a **Union** spy during the American Civil War (1861–1865). All those trips back and forth between the North and the South leading slaves to freedom made her very familiar with the land. She sometimes posed as a slave in her travels. She worked with a group of other former slaves and reported on the movement of the **Confederate** troops. Tubman also worked at times as a cook and a nurse.

SLAVERY AND THE CIVIL WAR

November 1860: Abraham Lincoln is elected president.

December 1860: Southern states announce they will secede, or separate, from the United States.

April 1861: The Confederate army attacks Fort Sumter in South Carolina, starting the Civil War.

January 1863: Lincoln issues the Emancipation Proclamation, which sets all slaves free in the Confederate states.

July 1863: The Union army wins a major battle at Gettysburg.

September – December 1864: Union general William T. Sherman captures Atlanta and Savannah in Georgia.

April 1865: Confederate general Robert E. Lee surrenders to Union general Ulysses S. Grant, effectively ending the war.

April 1865: Lincoln is assassinated.

December 1865: The 13th Amendment abolishes slavery.

In April 2016, the US Treasury Department announced that Harriet Tubman would replace Andrew Jackson on the front of the $20 bill.

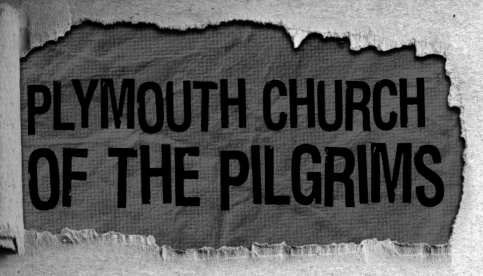

PLYMOUTH CHURCH OF THE PILGRIMS

Underground Railroad depots were hidden all over the country. Many were privately owned homes, but some were public buildings. One of these depots was the Plymouth Church of the Pilgrims in Brooklyn, New York. An Underground Railroad conductor named Charles B. Ray brought slaves to the Plymouth Church from Manhattan. The fugitives probably hid in the basement.

The minister of this church was Henry Ward Beecher. He was the brother of the author Harriet Beecher Stowe, who wrote the antislavery novel *Uncle Tom's Cabin*. Beecher was famous himself for his antislavery preaching. Every week about 2,500 people attended Plymouth Church to hear Beecher's sermons. Beecher encouraged people to resist slavery and disobey the Fugitive Slave Act. His sermons were printed and passed around.

REVEALED

Abraham Lincoln spoke out against slavery at the Plymouth Church of the Pilgrims in 1860. It's the only church in New York City he ever attended.

TRANSFER AT BROOKLYN

The Plymouth Church of the Pilgrims was known as Brooklyn's "Grand Central Depot" because it sheltered and cared for so many runaway slaves. Not only did the church welcome runaways, but Beecher encouraged his **congregation** to actively participate in and support the Underground Railroad. He wanted people to understand how terrible slavery really was. He occasionally held pretend slave **auctions** in the church to demonstrate slavery's cruelty.

This is a wood engraving by C. H. Wells showing what the Plymouth Church of the Pilgrims looked like in 1866.

FORT MONROE

Fort Monroe was a military base used as a depot in the Underground Railroad. Located in Virginia, it was one of the only Union-controlled military buildings in the South during the Civil War.

In 1861, slaves belonging to Confederate colonel Charles Mallory were working on Confederate military projects near the fort. They heard they were to be moved to North Carolina, further into Confederate territory. So, on May 23, they sought safety within Fort Monroe. General Benjamin F. Butler refused to send the slaves back to their owner, as the Fugitive Slave Act required. He said they were "**contraband** of war."

In August 1861, Congress passed the Confiscation Act, which allowed the Union to confiscate, or take, any property from the Confederates—and slaves were considered property.

REVEALED

Fort Monroe was known as the "Freedom Fortress."

WORKING AT THE FORT

Once the Confiscation Act was passed, thousands of slaves began traveling to Fort Monroe. By the time the war ended in 1865, over 10,000 had come to the fort for safety. These slaves worked there to earn their stay. This made some argue that the slaves weren't free, but had only changed masters. Even Harriet Tubman worked there. She was a nurse and also cooked and did laundry.

Fort Monroe was built as a coastal defensive post after the War of 1812.

DR. NATHAN THOMAS HOUSE

Dr. Nathan Thomas was the first doctor in Kalamazoo County, Michigan. His strong antislavery views led him to start a Michigan newspaper devoted to antislavery news. Between the years 1840 and 1860, Thomas and his wife Pamela Brown Thomas aided the Underground Railroad. Their home in Michigan was a depot for between 1,000 and 1,500 slaves. These slaves were eventually taken to Canada by way of Detroit.

The Thomases, who were Quakers, provided food, mended clothing, and treated the injuries of escaped slaves. Their work was done at night and in secret, but neighbors knew about it and even helped with food. Pamela Brown Thomas's **memoirs**, written in 1892, provided much information about their Underground Railroad activities.

REVEALED

Famous abolitionist Levi Coffin was sometimes called the president of the Underground Railroad. He directed activity on the "line" that included the Thomases' house.

TRAVELING THE QUAKER LINE

The slaves who came to the Thomases' house were "on the Quaker Line." This was the nickname for a series of depots in Michigan on the Underground Railroad. John Cross, a Quaker from Indiana, is thought to have been one of its organizers. He also **recruited** local "conductors" like the Thomases. Cross was so dedicated to the Underground Railroad that he earned the title "Superintendent," sheltering slaves at Wheaton College in Illinois where he was president.

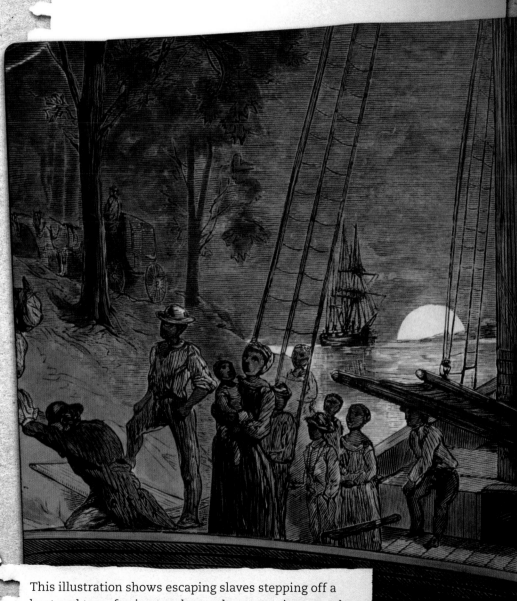

This illustration shows escaping slaves stepping off a boat and transferring to a horse-drawn carriage, another mode of transportation on their long route to freedom.

HENDERSON LEWELLING HOUSE

Salem was the first Quaker community in the state of Iowa. Henderson Lewelling moved there in 1837 with his brother to open a general store. Lewelling helped establish the Abolition Friends Monthly Meeting, which was attended by Quakers who not only opposed slavery, but also wanted to help fugitive slaves. Lewelling's house was home to the monthly Abolition Friends meetings as well as an Underground Railroad depot, welcoming slaves on their journey to freedom. Salem is only 25 miles (40 km) from Missouri, which was a slave state.

Hiding places were built into the house. There was a trapdoor leading to a hiding place for runaway slaves. A tunnel under the house connected to a basement fireplace, allowing fugitives to slip away easily when slave catchers arrived.

REVEALED

Lewelling and his brother were the first people to plant fruit trees in Iowa. He later moved to California and founded the community of Fruitvale. He's known as the Father of the Pacific Fruit Industry.

SOUTH OF THE BORDER

A well-known slave owner from Missouri, Ruel Daggs, came to Lewelling's house with armed men and threatened the residents and the entire town of Salem. Still, he was unsuccessful in getting his slaves back. According to the *Iowa Journal of History and Politics*, Daggs "finally realized the difficulty of holding slaves so near the free State of Iowa and **contemplated** selling his slaves south so that he would be free from the necessity of keeping a constant guard on valuable property."

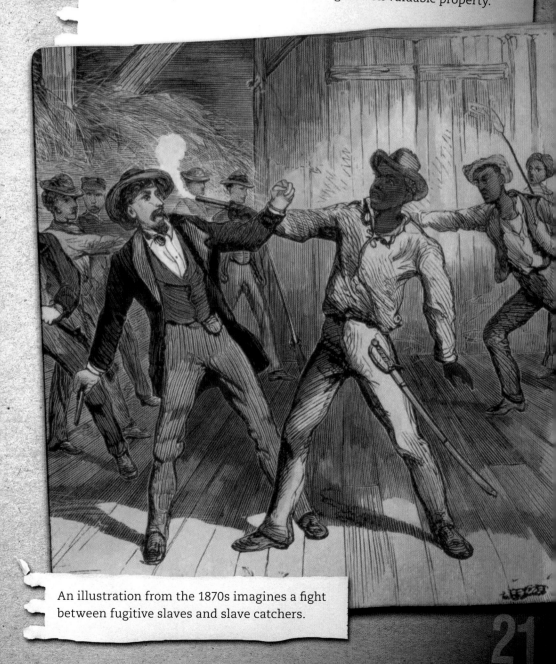

An illustration from the 1870s imagines a fight between fugitive slaves and slave catchers.

MILTON HOUSE

Joseph Goodrich was born in 1800 into a Massachusetts family that practiced the Seventh Day Baptist religion. Seventh Day Baptists were passionately against slavery. In 1838, Goodrich traveled to Wisconsin with other Seventh Day Baptists and founded the town of Milton. It was located near Rock River, a **tributary** of the Mississippi River—and a route for slaves escaping to Canada.

Goodrich built an inn called the Milton House around 1845, which was also a refuge for fugitive slaves. To avoid being seen by inn guests, escaped slaves entered his log cabin behind the inn. A trapdoor into the cabin's basement led to a tunnel that ran to the inn's basement. There, Goodrich supplied food and beds for the slaves.

REVEALED

The Milton House is the only part of the Underground Railroad in Wisconsin that is open to the public.

CRAWLING TO FREEDOM

The tunnel that ran from the Goodrich cabin to the inn was 3 to 5 feet (0.9 to 1.5 m) high and constructed after the inn was completed. The channel was so small that the escaped slaves would have had to crawl on their hands and knees in total darkness for 45 feet (13.7 m) from the basement of the cabin to the basement of the Milton House. This depot of the Underground Railroad *was* partially underground.

Part of the Milton House is shaped like a hexagon—meaning it has six sides.

GERRIT SMITH ESTATE

In 1835, abolitionist Gerrit Smith attended a conference in Utica, New York, where 600 antislavery supporters gathered at a church. A large group of **rioters** stormed the building during this gathering, forcing the meeting to end. Smith offered to host the meeting on his own estate in Peterboro, New York. These events led to Smith serving as the president of the New York Anti-Slavery Society between 1836 and 1839. During this time, he encouraged abolitionists to help slaves escape.

In the 1840s and 1850s, Smith was a stationmaster in the Underground Railroad, too. His estate was well known as a safe place for slaves on their way to Canada. It was also a financial and intellectual center of the antislavery movement.

REVEALED

Gerrit Smith's cousin was famous women's rights leader Elizabeth Cady Stanton.

UNDERGROUND GENEROSITY

Gerrit Smith was a generous man, often giving money to abolitionists for expenses and publications. It's estimated that he gave away over $8 million in his lifetime—which in today's money would be more than $1 billion! Smith saw his wealth as a gift from God that he should use to help others. He purchased individuals and families of slaves directly from slaveholders. Some thought he shouldn't give money to slaveholders, but rather give it to organizations that fought slavery.

Gerrit Smith (shown here) gave money to John Brown, who would raid a weapons storehouse in Harpers Ferry, Virginia, in 1859 in a failed attempt to start a slave rebellion.

NATHAN AND MARY JOHNSON
PROPERTIES

Not all depots on the Underground Railroad were the homes and businesses of white abolitionists. Nathan and Mary "Polly" Johnson were free black Quakers who lived in New Bedford, Massachusetts. They owned a whole block of properties and helped many escaped slaves, including famous abolitionist Frederick Douglass. The Johnson house was Douglass's first home after he escaped from slavery in 1838. Douglass wrote that Johnson "lived in a nicer house . . . was owner of more books, the reader of more newspapers . . . than nine-tenths of the slaveholders in Talbot County [Maryland]."

After Nathan left for the California Gold Rush in 1849, Polly housed at least one more fugitive slave. Polly helped pay for and maintain their properties in New Bedford by selling candy and cakes.

REVEALED
The Johnson house is now a National Historic Landmark.

WELCOMING COMMUNITY

In 1853, New Bedford had a higher population of African Americans than any other city in the Northeast. Almost 30 percent of these residents reported that they had been born in the South. The number of fugitive slaves ranged from 300 to 700. Some New Bedford schools and neighborhoods were **integrated**, which was unusual at that time. Additionally, Massachusetts was one of only five states that allowed blacks to vote. This attracted many free blacks and escaped slaves.

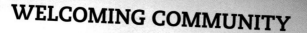

Frederick Douglass

The Johnsons' home is now home to the New Bedford Historical Society.

MORE DEPOTS TO DISCOVER

Today, we know of dozens of Underground Railroad depots. This book only names a few of these places and the brave individuals who offered them as shelter until slavery was finally abolished in 1865.

Many depots no longer stand, and doubtless, some depots weren't recorded at all. Their routes and the people who acted as conductors and stationmasters on them remain a secret. But because of these depots and people, thousands of slaves found their freedom.

Even today, Americans discover tunnels or trapdoors in their old homes and wonder if they live in a place that helped slaves on their way to freedom. Most will never know. However, a visit to an Underground Railroad depot can transport us back to experience the hidden history for ourselves.

REVEALED

Some historians estimate that about 100,000 slaves escaped using the Underground Railroad system.

ABOVEGROUND RAILROAD

Not all depots were quite so hidden. Many abolitionists were public with their views and actions despite the consequences. The governor of New York from 1839 to 1842, William Seward, openly supported the Underground Railroad and kept slaves hidden in his basement while serving as a senator. Some northern towns and cities even held bake sales to raise money to help the Underground Railroad, asking people to "buy for the sake of the slave"!

Monuments such as this one in Detroit, Michigan, honor the experiences of those brave enough to journey on the Underground Railroad.

GLOSSARY

abolitionist: one who fought to end slavery

auction: a public sale at which things are sold to people who offer to pay the most

Confederate: relating to the Confederate States of America, the states that left the United States during the American Civil War

congregation: an assembly or gathering of people, especially for a religious service

contemplate: to think deeply or carefully about

contraband: things that are brought into or out of a country illegally

exaggerate: to think of or describe something as larger or greater than it really is

integrate: to give races equal membership in something

memoir: a written account of the past in which someone describes personal experiences

recruit: to persuade someone to join some activity

rioter: one who behaves in a violent or uncontrolled way

tributary: a stream that flows into a larger stream or river or into a lake

Union: the Northern states during the period of the American Civil War

FOR MORE INFORMATION

BOOKS

Doak, Robin S. *Harriet Tubman*. New York, NY: Children's Press, 2016.

Lassieur, Allison, and Matt Doeden. *The Civil War Experience: An Interactive History Adventure*. North Mankato, MN: Capstone Press, 2013.

McDonough, Yona Zeldis. *What Was the Underground Railroad?* New York, NY: Grosset & Dunlap, 2013.

WEBSITES

American Civil War: Underground Railroad
www.ducksters.com/history/civil_war/underground_railroad.php
This website includes links to famous people involved in the Underground Railroad and the Civil War.

The Underground Railroad: Escape from Slavery
teacher.scholastic.com/activities/bhistory/underground_railroad/
Follow one man's journey from a plantation to freedom.

Avon Public Library

INDEX